An Illustrated Guide for Kids
A Journey Through Time with
the World's Most Famous Clock

Visit our author page for more children’s books
Amazon.com/author/88

By Nicole Damon

Welcome to the World of Big Ben!

Hello, young explorers! Have you ever heard the famous chimes of Big Ben? Maybe you've seen it in movies or pictures, standing tall and proud in the heart of London. Big Ben is not just a clock; it's a symbol of history, tradition, and the enduring spirit of the United Kingdom.

What is Big Ben?

Did you know the giant clock tower in London has a secret? Lots of people call it Big Ben, but that's actually the name of the Great Bell inside the tower! The tower where Big Ben lives is officially named the Elizabeth Tower, in honor of Queen Elizabeth II., but almost everyone calls it "Big Ben" because it's such a fun and catchy name!

Big Ben stands tall at the north end of the Palace of Westminster, and it's one of the most famous and recognizable landmarks in the whole world! It's not just a pretty face, though; it's a working clock that has been ticking away since 1859. That's over 160 years!

But Big Ben is more than just a clock. It's a symbol of the city of London and the United Kingdom. It has stood tall through wars, celebrations, and the changing times, always reminding people of the steady passage of time. In this book, we're going to explore the history of Big Ben, how it works, and some of the exciting stories that make it so special. So, grab your imaginary detective hats, and let's start our adventure into the world of Big Ben!

A Clock is Born

The History of Big Ben: Why and When It Was Built

Once upon a time, over 160 years ago, there was a magnificent palace in London called the Palace of Westminster. But something terrible happened – a great fire destroyed much of the palace in 1834. The people of London decided it was time to rebuild, and they wanted something grand and splendid to show the world how magnificent their city was. As part of the new design for the Palace of Westminster, it was decided that a giant clock tower should be built.

The construction of the clock tower started in 1843, and it took 16 long years to complete. Finally, in 1859, the great clock started ticking, and Big Ben's famous bongs were heard for the first time. The tower stood tall and proud, a symbol of the resilience and strength of London.

The Design: Who Designed Big Ben and What Inspired the Design

The design of Big Ben and the clock tower was a team effort. The architect Charles Barry was in charge of rebuilding the Palace of Westminster, and he came up with the idea of including a clock tower. However, it was Augustus Pugin who designed the beautiful gothic details of the tower that we admire today.

The clock itself was a masterpiece of engineering, designed by the lawyer and amateur horologist Edmund Beckett Denison, with the help of George Airy, the Astronomer Royal, and Edward John Dent, a famous clockmaker. Together, they created a clock that was not only beautiful but also incredibly accurate.

The design of the clock faces was inspired by the beauty and grandeur of the gothic style. Each face is over 7 meters in diameter, with 312 pieces of opal glass making up the clock face. The minute hands are over 4 meters long, and the numbers are about 60 centimeters tall. Can you imagine standing next to a number as tall as you are?

The tower itself was designed to be both beautiful and strong. It stands 96 meters tall, and its walls are over 3 meters thick at the base. The tower was built with a special kind of limestone called Anston, which gives it a lovely creamy color. And so, Big Ben was born, a magnificent clock in a splendid tower, ready to keep time for the people of London and become one of the most famous landmarks in the world.

Tick Tock Goes the Clock

How Does Big Ben Work?

Have you ever wondered what makes Big Ben tick? It's like a giant puzzle made of gears and wheels, all working together to keep the time. Let's take a peek inside the clock to see how it works! At the heart of Big Ben is a huge pendulum that swings back and forth. This pendulum is over 4 meters long and weighs as much as an elephant! Every time it swings, it makes the gears inside the clock move. These gears are connected to the clock's hands, making them go round and round.

But what keeps the pendulum swinging? It's a big weight called the "driving weight." This weight is pulled up high in the tower, and as it slowly comes down, it gives the pendulum the push it needs to keep swinging. It's like when you're on a swing, and your friend gives you a little push to keep you going.

To make sure Big Ben keeps the right time, there's a special person called the clock keeper who takes care of the clock. They wind up the driving weight and make tiny adjustments to the pendulum to keep it running smoothly.

The Famous Chimes:

The Story Behind the Famous "Bongs"

Now, let's talk about the part of Big Ben that everyone knows and loves – the famous "bongs"! Every hour, Big Ben chimes a melody that's known all over the world. But did you know that this melody has a special name? It's called the "Westminster Quarters."

The melody was created by a man named William Crotch in 1793, and it was chosen for Big Ben because it's simple and easy to hear from far away. The chimes are played on a set of bells inside the tower, with the biggest bell, Big Ben itself, ringing on the hour to mark the time.

But there's a fun story behind the first time Big Ben chimed. When the bell was first installed, it cracked during testing! So, they had to make a new bell, and this time, they made sure it was strong enough to last. The new Big Ben chimed for the first time on July 11, 1859, and it's been keeping time ever since. So, next time you hear the "bongs" of Big Ben, you'll know the amazing story of how this clock keeps ticking and chiming, day after day, year after year.

Big Ben Through the Ages

Important Events in Big Ben's History

Big Ben has been a silent witness to many important events in history. It has seen celebrations, wars, and changes, standing tall through it all.

One of the most dramatic moments in Big Ben's history was during World War II. In 1941, bombs fell on the Houses of Parliament, causing a fire. Firefighters bravely fought the flames, and Big Ben continued to chime throughout the night, a symbol of hope and resilience for the people of London.

Big Ben has also been part of many happy celebrations. Every New Year's Eve, people gather around the tower to hear Big Ben's chimes ring in the new year. The sound of the bell is broadcasted all over the country, and it's a moment of joy and excitement.

Renovations and Repairs: Keeping Big Ben Ticking

Even though Big Ben is a strong and sturdy clock, it needs a little help to keep ticking. Over the years, it has undergone several renovations and repairs to keep it in good shape. In 1976, Big Ben had a big scare. The clock mechanism broke, and the bell was silent for several months while repairs were made. It was a strange time for Londoners, who missed the familiar sound of the chimes.

More recently, in 2017, Big Ben went silent again for a major renovation. The tower, clock, and bells all needed some care and attention. The renovation included cleaning and repairing the clock faces, fixing the bell, and making sure the tower was safe and sound.

During this time, Big Ben only chimed on special occasions, like Remembrance Sunday and New Year's Eve. But don't worry, once the renovations are complete, Big Ben will be back to its regular chiming schedule, ready to keep time for many more years to come.

Inside the Tower

A Virtual Tour of the Elizabeth Tower

Let's take an imaginary trip inside the Elizabeth Tower, the home of Big Ben. The tower is like a tall, narrow house with many floors, each with its own secrets and stories. As we step inside, we start at the bottom and work our way up. The first thing we notice is the sound of our footsteps echoing in the stone stairwell. There are 334 steps to the top, so we better get going!

As we climb higher, we reach the clock room. This is where the magic happens! The room is filled with gears and wheels, all working together to move the clock's hands. It's like being inside a giant watch.

Finally, we reach the top, where the bells are. Big Ben is the biggest bell, and it's huge! It's about the size of a small car and weighs as much as 13 elephants. The other bells play the melody of the Westminster Quarters every quarter hour. From the top of the tower, we can see all of London spread out below us. It's a breathtaking view and a great reward for our climb!

Meet the Clock Keepers

Big Ben doesn't keep time all by itself. It has a team of dedicated people who take care of it, known as the clock keepers. The clock keepers have a very important job. They wind the clock three times a week, making sure it has enough power to keep going. They also check the pendulum and gears, making adjustments to keep the clock accurate.

But their job isn't just about mechanics. They also take care of the tower and the bells. They make sure everything is clean and in good condition, so Big Ben can continue to be a symbol of London for many more years.

Big Ben's Friends

The Houses of Parliament: Big Ben's Home

Big Ben is part of a very special building called the Houses of Parliament, also known as the Palace of Westminster. This is where the government of the United Kingdom makes important decisions and laws. The building is like a giant castle, with lots of towers, spires, and beautiful windows.

The Houses of Parliament sits right by the River Thames, which flows through the heart of London. From the river, you can see the whole building, with Big Ben proudly standing at one end. At night, the building is lit up, and it looks like something out of a fairy tale.

Inside the Houses of Parliament, there are grand halls, chambers, and corridors. Members of Parliament, also known as MPs, meet here to discuss important matters and make decisions for the country. It's a place full of history and important work, and Big Ben is right there to keep everyone on time.

Fun Facts and Records

Surprising Facts About Big Ben

Big Ben is full of surprises! Here are some fun facts that you might not know:

•**Big Ben is not the name of the tower.** As we learned earlier, Big Ben is actually the nickname for the Great Bell. The tower itself is called the Elizabeth Tower.

•**Big Ben's bell is really heavy.** The Great Bell weighs about 13.5 tons. That's as heavy as two adult elephants!

•**The clock faces are huge.** Each of the four faces of the clock is over 7 meters in diameter. That's taller than a giraffe!

•**There's a special light that shines when Parliament is in session.** At the top of the tower, there's a light called the Ayrton Light. It's turned on when the Houses of Parliament are meeting at night, so everyone knows that important decisions are being made.

•**Big Ben has its own coins.** In 2012, to celebrate the London Olympics, special 50p coins were made with a picture of Big Ben on them.

Records Held by Big Ben

Big Ben is not just famous; it's also a record holder:

•**Most accurate four-faced striking and chiming clock.** Big Ben is known for its accuracy, thanks to the skilled work of the clock keepers.

•**Largest four-faced chiming clock.** With its huge clock faces, Big Ben holds the record for being the largest clock of its kind.

•**Tallest free-standing clock tower.** When it was completed, the Elizabeth Tower was the tallest clock tower in the world.
•**First broadcast of its chimes.** On December 31, 1923, Big Ben's chimes were broadcast by the BBC for the first time, a tradition that continues today on special occasions. So, there you have it! Big Ben is not just a clock; it's a record-breaking, history-making icon that continues to amaze and inspire people all around the world.

Conclusion: The Significance of Big Ben

Big Ben isn't just a super tall clock tower in London, it's like a superhero for the whole city! It tells everyone the time, of course, but it's also a symbol of London, just like a special badge. it's a symbol of London and the United Kingdom, representing strength, history, and resilience.

It's a source of pride and inspiration worldwide, reminding us of the importance of time and marking moments in history. As a beacon for visitors, Big Ben brings people together, creating memories and sharing stories.

Looking ahead, Big Ben will continue to be a beloved symbol of London due to its timeless beauty, resilience, historical significance, and connection to people. As we bid farewell to Big Ben for now, let's remember its role as a friend, guardian, and storyteller, keeping time for us all, tick by tick, chime by chime.

Visit our author page for more children's books, and remember to follow us for updates on new releases, including illustrated storybooks, biography books, fun-fact picture books, coloring books, activity books for kids, and more:

Amazon.com/author/88

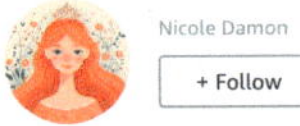

Nicole Damon

+ Follow

HOME ABOUT ALL BOOKS

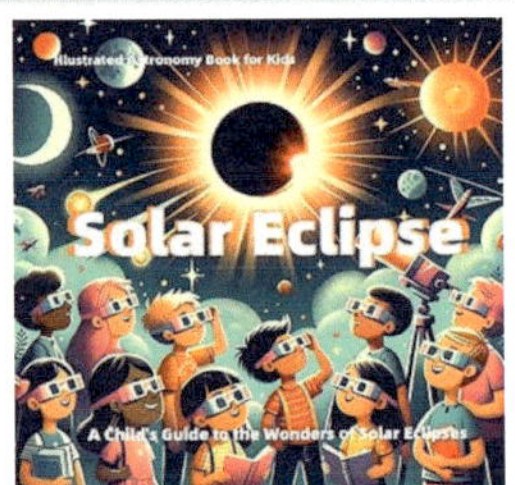

Quick look

for Kids: A Child's Guide to the Wonders...

Kindle Edition

$0.00 kindle unlimited

Other formats: Paperback

Quick look

for Young Explorers : Discover the Rich...

Part of: Illustrated Countries of the World for...

Kindle Edition

$0.00 kindle unlimited

Other formats: Paperback

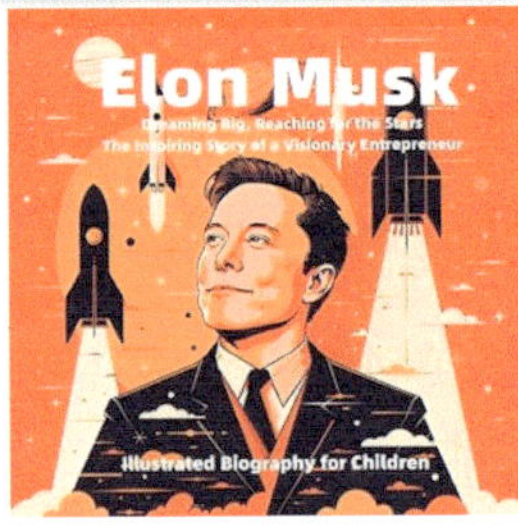

Quick look

Children: Dreaming Big, Reaching for the...

Part of: Illustrated Biographies for Children (12...

Kindle Edition

$0.00 kindle unlimited

or **$2.99** to buy

Other formats: Paperback

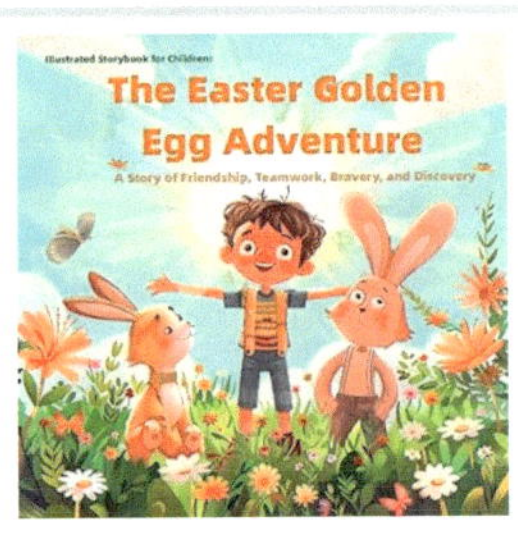

Quick look

Easter Golden Egg Adventure: A Story of...

Kindle Edition

$0.00 kindle unlimited

or **$2.99** to buy

Other formats: Paperback

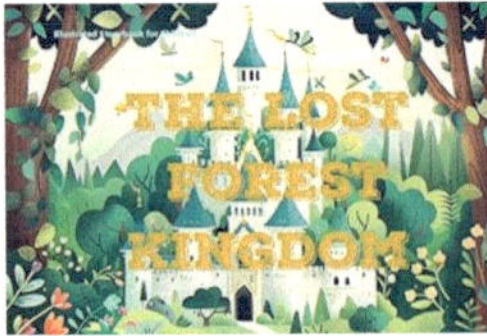

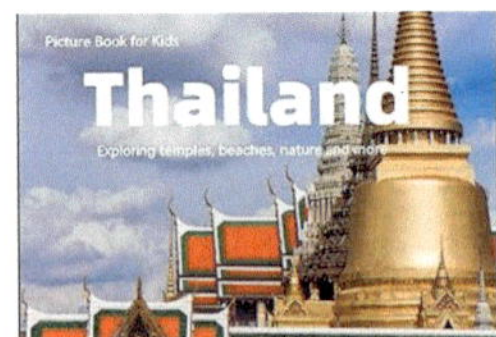

Made in the USA
Columbia, SC
26 June 2025